AURA

Life in 4D

by Dominic. J. Zenden

To Leona,
     with thanks for your help
Kind Regards
          Dominic J Zenden.

Published by WriterMotive
www.writermotive.co.uk

Foreword

Positive Aura Thinking is more than a concept, it is a reality.

My name is Dominic Zenden and ever since I was a child, I have been able to see auras around every single person and object. I would sit and watch in wonder as cotton candy clouds of colours swirled round people. The dictionary tells us the aura is a noun which means "a subtle emanation from flowers etc., atmosphere diffused by or attending a person, especially in mystical or spirit-ualistic use as a definite envelope of body or spirit."

Over the years, I discovered that not everyone saw the world in the same way as I did. Now I would like to share the knowledge I have learned over the past forty years. I believe that the aura you have shows many things about you, your thinking, the emotional state of your well-being, what food you eat and even areas where your body may have a weakness. All these are shown in your aura.

Many of you may be sceptical, but a good dose of healthy scepticism is always helpful in a world of con-flicting opinions. I have set this book out to explain the meaning of the aura. We explore the meanings of the colours and how to look beyond what a person tells us. Knowing about the aura will give us that extra edge.

Aura: Life in 4D

By first understanding how to see and then to interpret your own aura this book will take you step by step through your own personal journey of discovery.

You will be amazed when you start to see your own aura and how much better you will feel as your knowledge expands and you start to incorporate this new way of thinking into your life.

Mastering your own aura will teach you through personal experience that you have the ability to see the colour energy. When we meet people for the first time and knowing where to look, and how to focus, it all adds to your personal knowledge. When you start to read auras, it will open up a whole new world. A world that will lead to a better understanding of others, better relationships and stronger self-confidence.

Interested? By reading on, you may never look at people in the same light again.

Introduction

When you look around what do you see? The people we love, our friends, our possessions, the bright coloured flowers, emerald green grass, the shades of the seasons, golds, browns, pinks and whites. Colours are everywhere. Without colour, life would be just shades of grey, a bit like watching an old black and white television.

So what if I told you, you are missing out on even more colours? Amazing cotton candy clouds full of rainbow tones so rich in texture, but as delicate and fragile as china. These colours can help us decide some of the most important issues that we come across during our lifetime. Every single person, animal, plant, mineral or man-made object has a unique colour signature, even sounds have colours attached to them. Human voices give off different shades of every colour that you could ever imagine. These colours say so much about a person.

How do I know this? It's simple for as long back as I can remember I have been able to see what I have come to know as "The Aura." The colour energy field that every single object gives off through the level of vibration.

As a child, I never thought of the clouds of colours that swirled and hovered mixing different combinations, ballooning out of people, animals, and even aeroplanes as their exhaust fumes lit with pastel pinks and browns trailing behind as they roared across the horizon. In my world it was normal to watch streams of sound coming from people's mouths, it was natural to assume everybody had the same vision. As I grew, I came to understand that what I saw wasn't the same as my family and friends. The world I lived in was a colourful mixture of sound and colour. I learnt fast what different combinations of colours meant especially around voices. The pitch and tone dictated the colours. Angry voices would be very dark, blacks crimsons would jump in jagged fragmented daggers. Emotional voices would be pink, light red with blue purple edging almost stopping before the flow of colour floated out of the mouth and into the air. Happy laughter would be light yellow with blobs of orange and so on. The colours in the voice don't always match the aura surrounding the person. So for me it was so easy to see if people were being false or genuine.

Now I'm very interested in helping you find your own colours around people. Just think of the advantage this would give you when trying to work out your personal relationships. Just by being able to read a person's aura you could interpret the person's personality, match your auras for compatibly without speaking. It's real and not that hard once you know where to look.

The other side to auras is you can work on your own. So much we do in life is by instinct. Our senses work alongside us almost invisibly without us realising. Smell is a great example. We can be taken back instantly to our youth by the smell of cut grass. This is because our mind link memories to our senses. Our aura reflects how we are feeling inside. If our aura is tucked up close to our body, it's a very defensive or fearful energy that we give out. Others will by instinct pick up on this and avoid us. Not much good if we are single, looking for love. Or wanting that job interview to go well. We can change our auras by how we think, feel and live again it's not that difficult. Training what we show to people is the very thing that we learn from a very early age. We now have to understand the colours we give out, the meaning of those colours, training our thoughts to give us the best possible chance of achieving the best outcomes from what we set out to do.

Your aura says so much about you. Get it right and life has a way of becoming uncomplicated.

Dominic Zenden
hello@dominiczenden.com
www.dominiczenden.com
Twitter@dominiczenden
Facebook Dominic.J.Zenden

Little miracles happen every day.

To Alison

Chapter Breakdown

learning how to look rather than listen to what people are saying).

Chapter Six: Photographic Auras

(What is a photographic aura? How do we see and then read these auras? How we can use this knowledge to improve the way we see others who we might not have met in person).

Chapter Seven: Better Relationships

(Everything we ever needed to know about auras and relationships. Working with the colours in others aura's to build knowledge of how certain feelings and emotions can affect the way we feel. Understanding how positive mental thinking can change the way we think and how others perceive us).

Chapter Eight: Spiritual Auras

(Positive aura thinking is a state of mind that affects the way our aura shows how we are feeling to others. This is a way of thinking that we allow the reader to feel good about how they are feeling, the colours they are wearing and the people who are attracted to them).

Chapter Nine: New Knowledge

(Using all the new knowledge in the book to start a positive way of life. Recapping on aura reading, stating the benefits of being able to see auras. How all this fits into a brand new way of seeing others).

Chapter Ten: Last Word

(Summary of what the message of Positive Aura Thinking means. Notes from the author on how he came about writing this book and the effect of seeing auras has had on his life).

Chapter One: The Aura

(The purpose of this chapter is to help a novice understand what an aura is, how to affect your personal aura in a positive way. This knowledge should allow the reader to make much better informed decisions when choosing friends, personal relationships.)

Our aura is as much a part of our body as our arms, legs and our own personal thoughts. In fact, the aura will give away how we are feeling emotionally, physically and mentally.

The signals our aura sends out to others can be picked up affecting who we attract as well as who we may wish to attract.

Our aura will reflect the state of thinking we have, helping us create the world we believe we live in.

Our thoughts become what builds the world around us through our aura.

Thoughts become things. The aura just magnifies those thoughts so others can instinctively feel our personal needs and moods.

Creating a positive aura will in turn be more attractive to other positive people.

Those who have dealt with their own issues don't need another to facilitate them, this means they are free to enjoy life.

So often when we don't have personal direction we look to others.

By helping them we forget our own difficulties, but those difficulties remain in our thoughts so in turn show out in our aura.

If we believe our path in life is to mend others, we will attract people who are emotionally damaged.

Like will attract like.

An example of this is the person who wishes to meet a partner, but has no idea how to start.

The aura will show out confusion, mistrust, emotional need so guess what type of person this person will meet.

The whole circle will go round and round creating even more havoc until they come to the conclusion all they attract is emotionally difficult people.

Changing our aura can make all the difference in the world. It's amazing, get the aura right, life follows.

So now we understand how having a positive aura can change the way we create our friendships we now need to understand how the aura works.

Everything in your body vibrates at a certain frequency, your mind, your vital organs, even your blood as it rushes around your body, giving off a vibration of sound.

Your voice gives out so many different colours, as you talk unaware of the flow of salmon pinks, deep reds and blues.

Anything that you take into your body affects the colours and the tone of the aura.

People that drink coffee or other caffeine rich drinks have an eerie lime green showing out from the inner edge of their aura.

The deeper the green, the more regular their intake.

This will show up other areas of the aura that can pinpoint why the person has a need to keep topping up with artificial energy boosts.

The aura is not only an indicator of lifestyle, but also is a cocoon of light that protects our inner body from damage.

The outer aura reacts as a buffer against the invisible things that we don't see.

Human viruses and other people's negative energies and so on.

Aura: Life in 4D

People who feel low will often have holes in their aura that will let energy out and negative energy in.

This is why when we are feeling low or lacking in drive it can be down to our own personal energy leaking away from us, being replaced by negative feelings or illness.

When we have a healthy aura, these holes won't occur.

Or won't occur as quickly.

Being around difficult people or stressful situations can take its toll too.

We all know how we feel when our job becomes too much to cope with, or our best friend needs a lift by sucking the energy out of us.

This is just an extension of our aura being weakened.

If we don't replace this energy by ourselves or by our understanding, then the outer aura becomes thin then holes will appear.

So how do we stop this happening?

Like any part of our body, we need first to be aware of the effects that living will have on it.

Every single day we live our life beside others.

Allowing others to come too close on our emotional feelings can affect the way our aura is.

We take on the feelings from people who are only too glad to pass them over.

I call these people energy vampires.

They will attach then suck the energy they need then move on or away until they need their next feed. Recognising these people is your first move away from allowing emotionally difficult people into your life. We will often allow these people in when we don't have our own identity.

We feel if we help others it will save us from ourselves, giving a purpose to our own life.

This is such false thinking.

We start to believe unless others are happy we couldn't be.

Not only does that allow others to take from our own stores of energy they will keep coming back for more. So how we feel about ourselves is so very important. Far more than we ever realise.

Our whole life is affected by our relationships, the people who we invite into our inner self.

Aura: Life in 4D

By valuing who we are, we would never let needy people lower our own self-esteem in order to keep us with them because of their need to feed off our aura.

The outer aura is the first place to work on.

A good strong positive energy field wrapped around us will not only stop us from being drawn into situations it will also retain the energy we have, thus eliminating the need for artificial energy such as caffeine, sugar and fast foods.

Living is a consent battle against taking the short or the long way round.

We have to find a middle ground. It's no good being an all or nothing person.

Fitting into our routine the things that can help us is the basis of making our lives' the best they can be.

The aura is a reflection on our lifestyle.

Making times to do certain things will help us.

For instance. Having a bath is such a small part of our daily life.

In busy times, we would tend to shower.

Our aura being an extension of our body needs to be refreshed; bathing is a very simple way of washing away any negative energy that may be attached.

Showering doesn't clear this energy; we miss certain parts of our bodies allowing these areas to build up in negative attachments.

People who shower show collections of dark energies around the back of their legs and the sides of their torso.

Certain nature oils dropped into bath water will also help the aura mend itself, closing the holes that can be worn into our aura during daily life.

I have found orange oil very good at mending the outer shell; this is the most vulnerable part of the aura.

It's like the protective shell of an insect.

Or the enamel on teeth.

Two or three drops of orange oil in your bath water will over a few weeks close up and strengthen the outer aura.

The benefits of this will be feeling less tired.

The energy the aura holds will stay around the body.

The need for artificial stimulants becomes less; the need to over eat through tiredness becomes unnecessary. So by one simple process you already have the knowledge that will help you create the feelings of well-being.

This is turn will help you with the middle aura.

This is the part of the aura that dictates your emotional well-being.

How you're thinking and feeling.

These are the colours that people pick up from us when they are in need.

The brighter the middle colours, the easier it is to connect with like-minded people.

So people with bright middle colours will attract liked minded people who have no need to live their lives' through others.

This is an enhancing person who will be able to cope with life's up and downs without going into extremes.

When we feel unwell or emotionally unbalanced our middle aura becomes pale, diluted into pastel colours, weak and airy.

People with weak middle colours are often not able to deal with situations, asking others to make choices or blaming others for the difficulties they are facing.

Will try many ways of cheering themselves up by spending money, eating sugary foods or attaching to alcohol, even helping others in order to forget how they might be feeling.

All these things will act as a trap and slowly tighten around themselves.

Creating more need is a circle that when cut takes a little getting used to.

The benefits however far outweigh being trapped in an ever decreasing circle.

Positive mental thinking can change so much of our middle aura. Later in this book I will share some insights on the middle aura.

The inner aura is all about the food we eat and drink, the clothes we wear and how we see ourselves.

The other part of this is any discomfort we may feel from injuries, illness and likely areas that are susceptible to being damaged easier than other parts of our bodies.

I will go into detail about the inner aura in later chapters but for now it's enough to know we can work on our inner aura to allow ourselves to feel the best we can be, perform in sport even better, make better choices in people and increase the confidence that we feel inside.

Having a healthy aura is an amazing feeling.

Aura: Life in 4D

Once we have mastered our own then we can learn how to read the colours that come from others.

Aura Wisdom

You can be anything you want to be.

Chapter Two: Seeing Auras

How much do we really see?

We go from one moment to the next without taking too much notice of our surroundings.

A simple test is to recall what people around us were wearing.

Can you remember what colours your boss was dressed in?

Or the colour of your partner's clothes? We are so consumed by how we are feeling, failing to notice others.

It's true.

How many women are pre-occupied by make-up or hair styles?

We are all at it.

It seems nobody notices anyone else we are all too busy looking at ourselves.

So how can we change this in order to notice what is right in front of us, the colours everybody gives out.

Aura: Life in 4D

I have never come across anyone other than myself who can see auras.

This doesn't mean nobody can, I just haven't met them yet.

Like anything in life we can learn to pick up on the signs, become aware of how to interpret the energy and start to pick up the colours that come from every single object. It's knowing where to start.

So much to learn but wanting to know everything.

We want to see auras instantly.

Our knowledge of the aura is very limited.

We know it's a part of who we are.

We also know it's the energy that surrounds the body.

Most of us know it comprises of different shades of colours.

These colours indicating how we feel.

But how do we start to see first our own aura then the aura of others?

Seeing is believing.

The aura first needs to be seen so you can trust that if you work hard it will be worth it, like anything we have a limited attention span so don't try too hard at first.

Short bursts of practise are far better than continuous long periods of staring ahead.

So when you start limit yourself to ten to fifteen minutes.

This can be built up over a few weeks, but I know once you start seeing aura's you will want to see even more.

To start with you will need a few simple things.

A blackboard or a dark background.

This will help you see the outline.

When you become more focused, you won't need a dark background.

Start with a potted plant.

Plants have amazing auras and unlike people don't move, complain or need the toilet!

You will also need some cut flowers.

This will help you see how the aura changes as the flowers die.

Aura: Life in 4D

This might sound cruel, but believe me once you start seeing aura's you will think it's what you want to see. A changing aura will show you that you're seeing something different every day and it's not your imagination.

Plant auras are very delicate.

Very soft colours, so you need to find yourself a table with no direct light, away from windows without curtains.

If you think about light, the more light you have around you the harder it is to see outlines.

You can't see a torch in daylight.

A dimly lit room is best to start with.

Put the blackboard or dark background behind the plant.

Then close your eyes for about a minute, (use this time to focus your mind on what you're about to do.)

Then open both eyes and look at one part of the plant.

A flower or a leaf is the best place to start with.

After a few moments, you will start to see a pale outline.

It's normally green or white when you first see it.

Once you have the outline of the area you're looking at, take your focus out slightly to include more of the plant until you can see the mist all around your plant.

As your eyes get more and more used to seeing the mist, you will start to pick up on colours and different depths of colour.

Each plant has a different feel to it, but the focus is the same.

Remember a dimly lit room is the best way to get your eyes adjusted.

Now try the cut flowers.

Place the vase in front of your dark background, and go through the same procedure.

Set everything up then close your eyes, focus for about a minute, then look directly at one flower before moving your gaze out to whole vase.

This time you could see a change in the colours of the aura.

If the flowers are fresh, you will see the outline in pale light colours.

Whites, greens, yellows are common colours that you will pick up on.

Aura: Life in 4D

If the flowers are a few days old you will start to see the colours fade, the whites will start becoming grey, then darker grey, then light black before turning a deep black.

It's good for you to see the change over a few days. Watching a flower die isn't something we do every day, it can only be experienced when you start to open up to the colour fields around the object.

It will give you a different way of looking at cut flowers.

So now you have had your first glimpse of a living aura.

It's amazing.

You will never look at the world in the same way again.

But after a while you will start to look all around your local area.

You will see plants in a totally different way.

Even grass becomes interesting.

The emerald green aura is unlike any other shade of green that I have ever seen.

Remember the colours you are seeing are created, by the energy of the plant vibrating at different pitches, thus creating colours.

Every living object has its own vibrational pitch.

This includes minerals, water and the gases we breathe.

Now you see plant auras, the next step is to start looking at bigger plants and animals, before we move onto people.

Tree's and animals are a major part of the world we live in.

From the birds in the garden to the pets we live with.

For this next part, having a pet of your own will help.

But it's not essential.

But you will have to seek out a tree and animals in your local area.

I have found parks fantastic places to study auras.

All forms and levels of life congregate there.

Sunset is the best time to start attuning your eyes.

At the beginning finding out where to look will help, dimly lit areas allow you to find the outline of the aura. Starting with smaller tree's focus your eyes in the same way as you did with the pot plant and flowers.

Standing far enough away to see the whole tree (remember you're starting small, a five to six foot tree is ideal.)

Aura: Life in 4D

Look at one area first then gradually allow your eye's to open up to see the whole tree.

This might mean you walking backwards, so before you start just make sure your backwards path is clear, so you can move back a few steps if necessary.

This might take a few goes.

The dark sky in the background will help. Later when you have found your focusing point you won't need the dark sky backdrop.

The rewards are truly wonderful.

Trees have some amazing colours, each tree has a different feel and as you progress to larger older tree's you will start seeing the colours getting deeper and deeper.

You will notice so much more.

Trees are full of life.

Squirrel's running up then down, insects that buzz around the branches, birds with bright coloured voices, all emit a light colour signature.

Picking up on the kaleidoscope of colours opens up another world.

Please don't give up if nothing is happening for you.

Like mediation, some can with ease, some take a little while to get the hang of focusing.

But most achieve.

You're not trying to find something, it's already there, it's just a case of teaching yourself something new.

Mastering auras will help you in so many different ways,

You have now come a long way.

From knowing a little about aura's, to seeing aura's around plants, you know that the aura is a unique colour signature that surrounds every single object that we see.

By choosing to look at a deeper level, it's now time to move onto people with a little help from our pets.

What do we want to get from our new found skill?

Do we want just to marvel at the wonders of the universe seeing colours where we only used to see dull familiar objects?

I doubt this would be enough.

What we want is to be able to work out what others may be thinking or who is compatible to us.

Aura: Life in 4D

What does this man's aura tell me about him?

Can I trust him?

The questions are never ending.

But one step at a time.

Just because you can play chopsticks on the piano doesn't mean you are about to play Mozart.

Taking one step forward is all about learning one piece at a time.

Let's first try our skills on an animal.

Have a good look at your pet whilst they are sleeping.

(If you don't own an animal borrow one!)

The hardest thing we do is focus. Animals move around so does the energy field around them.

If we can get them to stay in one place long enough, we can learn where to focus.

About ten centimetres above the back of head is the best place to start.

A dark blanket or background will help you; the outline of an animal is very similar to that of a person.

The aura has three different levels.

The outer aura is what you will see first.

Light orange is the first colour, followed by pale yellow and light grey, then white turning to very pale pink the closer to the animal that you look.

Animals have very simple aura's that reach out about ten centimetres, if happy and content. It's good to see what a basic healthy aura looks like.

(Very few humans have a basic healthy aura.)

Knowing this makes it easier to interpret human auras later on.

Your pets' aura will change from time to time, when hungry, or tired, excited or upset all of these basic emotions exist in our animals.

Keep watching them during their daily routine you will soon pick up on the colour changes.

Before too long you won't be even thinking about looking.

You will automatically react to what you are seeing.

This should give you a brand new understanding of your pet.

You now have the basic knowledge you need to start looking at human auras.

Aura: Life in 4D

This is where we start having to work a little more.

People don't stand still.

They talk, often using language to disguise how they are feeling.

It takes on a different feel when you are hearing one thing yet seeing another in their aura.

We have to learn to trust what we are seeing, not hearing.

Peoples' auras are complicated.

When we first start reading human auras we need all the help we can get.

The outer aura is very much the same in all people. An orange shell. So if we first look for the orange this will guide us towards the depth.

The same things apply to humans as apply to plants, trees and animals.

The more alive we are, the brighter the colours.

When you first look at a person's aura try to start with a younger person.

These auras are very often similar to that of our pets.

It's only as we get older the aura becomes full of attachments, or holes, children may have an untainted view on life until about seven years old.

The orange outer aura is light pastel the energy inside light grey or white with touches of blues and yellows with very pale pink inner aura.

Of course, children vary.

But once you have the ability to see the aura your knowledge of how to read the colours will follow.

The same method applies.

Focus your thoughts.

Allow your eyes to adjust, focus on one small part of the person.

An arm or a hand. Then open up your sight to the whole of the person.

Because we are all humans, there are two exercises we can practise on ourselves.

The first exercise is to feel the depth of aura.

Take your left hand and hold it flat out in front of you, palm up.

Take your right hand and hold it over your left hand, palm down.

Now move your right hand slowly away in an upward direction.

What you will feel is the heat of your aura coming from your left hand.

The heat will start off hot and get cooler as the right hand moves further away.

When the heat stops that's the outer part of your aura.

Try this a few times it will get you used to feeling the energy and the depth your aura has around your hands.

Now hold your right hand out in front of you. Close your eyes and focus open both eyes and fix your gaze on the tip of your middle finger.

Again it helps when you first start to use a black background.

You should see a white glow around the tip of your finger.

The more you practise this, the sooner you will start to see the white light splitting into colours, like looking at light passing through a prism.

By now everything you have learned will be coming to-gether, you are now ready to take your skills into the world you inhabit.

Next it's time to prepare you to what you may see in others and how to interpret what the different colours mean.

Aura Wisdom

Every single thing you ever do starts with a single thought.

Chapter Three: Working On Your Aura

What do you have the power to change in your life today?

I talk to many people who all tell me "I'm trying to change". But by that dreaded phrase I just know that change is as far away from them as it was in the beginning.

Some of us get so used to being in our own unhappy place it's easier to stay put.

If we stay the same then life is just about what we thought it would be fulfilling our prophecies.

I have a different way of thinking. The moment, it's the only time we have is the moment we are in right now.

So trying to change infers that tomorrow we will start, but if we start in the now then every moment counts and tomorrow becomes a distant thought.

That's the first phrase of change.

Everything we ever are or will ever do starts with one single thought.

How we think is what we become.

Understanding where our thoughts come from can also help us with the way we think.

If you believe that thought only comes from us, then you may be interested in thinking about this.

I have come to see thought in a different way.

I believe that thoughts come at us from different directions.

Not only do we start our own thinking but our past lives, our future lives, our mentors or spirit guides all have an input into the way we think.

Have you ever woken up thinking of something totally different to when you went to sleep?

Where did that thought come from?

It wasn't you. It's very common.

Some of the best writers, poets, inventors have all woken up in the morning with the next big thing in the middle of their head.

A certain famous song writer openly admits that a lot of his lyrics he had dreamt the night before.

This is only one example of an outside influence that occurs in your thoughts.

As soon as we realise this it opens us up to all the knowledge that we want to understand.

We have a choice, we can separate our thoughts, listen then act or we can just stay with what we are told. I know which way I choose.

So how can thought change our aura?

We must look at our aura as an extension of our body.

Once we accept this, then it's the beginning of understanding that our inner thoughts affect the way our aura is. The outer aura is the proactive shell that stops negative energy penetrating the rest of our aura. If we believe that we can't think that our lives will become the lives we so want to live this very negative thought process weakens the very strong outer aura.

I believe that personal negative thinking is one of the major factors in our outer aura becoming weak.

We will surround ourselves with people who need us.

Make others responsible for our happiness.

What we don't see is the energy leaking away from us filling up the aura of others. Have you ever thought why you feel so drained when you are around certain people?

The aura is like a giant person sized balloon that extends all the way round us.

If you think of a deflated balloon that is what you will see when you look at negative minded people.

Without you blowing it back up for them with your energy, these people become depressed or attached to an addiction.

Asking why those people are in your life is a good start to changing the way you think in order to protect your outer body which in turn strengthens the outer aura.

When I look at a person who has good self-esteem, a positive outlook on life the outer aura is a strong orange which can extend up to ten centimetres thick around the top of the head.

These individuals stand out. As soon as they walk into a room you can sense you're in the presence of a person who has command of the space they occupy.

You rarely see these people with needy people. They surround themselves with strong can do people. Like attracts like.

So the first step to a positive natural aura is to believe it can be so.

Thought become things.

When we have a positive mental outlook, we will manifest what we are thinking.

That's getting the thought process right.

This is the foundation on which we can build.

The next stage is to get our lifestyle right.

To build a strong aura which we have come to understand is an extension of who we are, thinking about what we put into our bodies is totally our responsibly.

What we eat, drink and even smoke affects the whole aura.

When we are overweight, it's because another area of our life isn't right.

When we're feeling good, we don't look to food.

The expression comfort eating is just that.

We don't need that packet of crisps or those biscuits but because the energy is leaking away from us it easy to reach for the quick fix food.

When we plan what we eat and drink we get it right.

A few minutes writing a list before we shop, planning meals around long lasting slow release foods is not that hard.

Supermarkets want us to buy the high-profit lines, chocolate, cakes, fizzy drinks these are all so available right in front of you at easy reach.

Taking time to shop can change your aura.

Having a knowledge of the places you can buy food is invaluable.

How many of us go once a week to a large supermarket get everything we need and much we don't before coming home unpacking then sitting in front of the telly with a newly brought pizza exhausted.

All the time that we have saved is spent watching the latest episode of the soap we have been following for weeks.

This is meaningless.

We might as well be robots.

No feelings just commands.

How many of us enjoy shopping? Not many.

We have lost the art of shopping in many different shops.

We don't have the time. Not true. We only think it is.

Aura: Life in 4D

Changing your aura is about changing your thinking. To change the way you shop is about changing how you see your life, your routine, and your needs.

Can you imagine how much fun it is to shop at the local market?

Fresh food locally sourced.

Just replacing the time we lay in bed or watch television or sit around can make this part of our life again.

I know not everyone will think the same as I do, but just think about it like social networking in person. Supermarkets are the sausage factory of food shopping.

If you want to live your life by command, your aura will reflect this.

Just ask yourselves one question.

"What do we do with all the time we save?"

It's not only what we eat but how we think about what we take in.

The aura reflects every single thing we put into our bodies and in turn will attract others who take the same things into their bodies.

If we look at this how many couples that you see who have been living together for over a year look the same?

This is no accident.

They have the same lifestyle.

I will often see couples in the same style coats walking around shopping the same foods week in week out, it's something you would see anywhere in the world.

As humans, we don't like having to think. We live by numbers.

To change your aura, it's about how much thought you put into your life.

The foods you buy.

How you buy them and how willing you are to put effort into what you want to achieve.

We have now discussed how to start the process of changing the aura you have. The next thing to consider is the colours we surround ourselves with.

The clothes we wear.

What makes us decide on what we wear?

So many factors are involved. Our job, what we are doing that moment.

How we wish to feel.

Aura: Life in 4D

What signals we want others to see from us?

So many areas to consider.

I would like to start with what we choose to wear when we don't have any restrictions.

Believe it or not the colour of our clothes more often than not matches the colour of the aura we have.

Just recently I had a meeting with a man that I had never met before.

He dressed in grey.

That was so him.

No energy in his aura, all he was interested in was himself.

The poor man didn't have enough energy to give it away.

But when he had prepared for our meeting he hadn't gone out to show how he was feeling it was done without thought, totally unconscious of what his aura was saying.

You will often see men dressing in grey suits or dark clothing but will wearing red or brightly coloured socks.

This is a person that wants to break free of convention.

Doesn't want to rock the boat, but wants to feel able to express how he is feeling without any outward signs. The bright socks show deep down that their emotional self is unfulfilled.

Next time you're sat on a train or bus just have a look around it's amazing how we express our true self but not to the world. The colours we feel comfortable in are an extension of how we are feeling. Were we get this wrong is by thinking if we put a red scarf on or a bright blue jumper it will change our moods.

All that does is disguise how we are feeling.

It changes nothing.

Working on the foods we eat, our daily routine, exercise and our emotional self-changes the colours that surround us.

We can then feel the colours we wear.

Our subconscious dictates how we shop.

Many of us will buy the same coloured clothes over and over again, purely because like food shopping we don't put much thought into why we buy.

We just buy.

An example of this which everyone can relate to is the person who wakes up feeling down, not knowing what to do goes out shopping.

Needing to feel better they buy an item of clothing one size to small in bright orange.

The person feels loads better, but the item is put in the wardrobe at the back never to be worn, as a reminder that instead of being a size smaller is a size bigger than they want to be every time the item catches the eye.

We all do this. It's a shortcut to feeling better, but it's also a long way round to feeling down.

If you were to look at all your clothes right now how many of them do you really wear?

We stay with the items we feel comfortable wearing.

The colours don't change that much.

Another thing about what we wear.

We dress to impress, at work, going out, even when we are at home.

But this is hard work, getting up every day trying to match our clothes to our activities.

When we have a stable relationship one that we can re-lax in without judgement we dress how we want too, baggy tracksuit bottoms loose fitting jumpers items of clothes that have become familiar, old friends that we know and trust to hide the bumps, we then relax.

When a relationship gets to this stage it's the biggest of compliments to the person you're sharing your life with, it means that the person you're with is with you for who you are, not what you're showing out.

Couples that feel close will often dress alike not always in public but in the privacy of their own home. Every single thing we buy has a story attached to it; it's like looking back at a history of our life.

Changing the clothes we wear doesn't change our lives.

Changing our mind-set does.

Aura Wisdom

Never wait if it's wrong today it will be wrong tomorrow.

Chapter Four: Meaningful Colours

The whole world is full of colour.

Who doesn't like watching the sun rise or set?

The beautiful colours blend into one another creating new even more wondrous colours.

The food we eat is only appealing because of the colours we see before we eat.

Colours mean so much to all of us.

The colours of the aura are even more remarkable.

Once your eyes and mind are tuned into picking up the colours of the aura you will never watch another sunrise in the same way. Watching people, animals, even plants will be just as amazing.

But what do the colours of the aura mean?

How can we interpret the mixtures of the cotton candy swirls that flow from the body?

In this chapter I will attempt to explain the meanings of the different colours, then the combinations of colours that you might see. Understanding the meanings will help you work out what you are looking at and how this knowledge will help you in your daily life to make good decisions when interacting socially and personally.

Dark Blue

Is often seen in the middle aura. It's all about communication; people who have dark blue are very strong in their use of language, make good debaters.

These people are stubborn believing their views are the right ones.

Blue

Very person based. Would love to share views, help others.

Open to new ideas and to change. People who have blue middle auras will work as writers, teachers, have a very clear view of right and wrong, very rarely do they step out of line preferring to take the safe secure route through life.

Make good partners, but can be dull.

Light Blue

A light blue aura is all about living in a fantasy world.

These people will have their heads in the clouds, day dreamers. Non-confrontational, very laid back approach to any problems.

Aura: Life in 4D

Make good friends but not that ambitious.

Dark Red

Impulsive. Unpredictable.

Can easily become addicted to frills, would live for the moment.

Would take risks without thought.

Can have anger issues from past mistakes.

Dark red auras can be very attractive people, it's easy to see why others would want to be around these people, but dangerous, only loyal to themselves.

Red

Can be hard to understand, would start off relationships fast not wanting partners to see too far into them.

Passionate to extreme.

Past issues will play apart in emotional decisions.

Can be loners in life not trusting other people's judgement.

Would have low self-esteem, need reassurance on a regular basis.

Most red people have issues with others, but keep them well below the surface until they feel safe.

Light Red

Light red auras are very rare; these people have no passion about life.

Will stay alone often choosing very few friends.

People, who don't make decisions, tend to stay where they feel safe. Not easy to get on with.

Can lack social skills, I believe this is why you don't come across light red auras.

Dark Pink

Dark pink auras are mixtures of emotions.

People who have not worked out their own sexuality or are very confused over emotions.

Have an outward going personally can be very loud and in your face type, which when you first meet them can be overwhelming.

You would never be bored, but you might never feel that safe, life would be full of ups and downs.

Pink

Good balance, would love life, outgoing, social.

Have a strong approach to achieving.

Never be fooled by a pink aura, even though the person would come across as less than knowledgeable these people have always done their homework.

They make great partners in life and business never asking anyone to do something that they wouldn't.

Honest, straight forward with an edge. Hard to fall out with unless your unreasonable.

Light Pink

Not so driven but personality would be good.

Would prefer to be lead. Loyal, kind and gentle. Life would be fun childlike at times.

Sense of humour very few confrontational moments.

Dark Green

When you look at a person who drinks a lot of caffeine what you see is green, it also comes from alcohol cigarettes, artificially colourings sugar and even too much fat in the diet.

People with dark green auras eat too much of the quick fix foods and will be drawn to stimulants, tending to have gaps in the outer aura.

Green

Not as strong as above but with green it's the wrong balance in the diet.

Too much tea, coffee or coke; not enough exercise.

People who spend their day sitting down have green inner auras.

Light Green

I don't see many adults who have light green it's mainly children, animals and plants.

I believe the air that we breathe is light green.

When we have very little else polluting our bodies, this colour will show up. Very line green in an aura only shows up when I see people who live away from civilisation.

Orange

The outer aura.

What you are looking for is a strong outer aura.

Bright orange with a glow is the sign of a fit and healthy person.

It's also one of the easiest colours to pick up on because everyone has an orange outer aura

Aura: Life in 4D

Yellow

Very open, easy to be around.

People who have a yellow inner aura are at peace with themselves.

Have found who they are and willing to share knowledge with others.

Dark Yellow

Knowledge seekers.

Dark yellow or gold is about finding truths.

Often these people will like to travel, have an interest in how others live.

Teachers, spiritual healers and peacemakers.

Seeing yellow in the inner and outer aura is very often a person who has grown enough not to judge others.

The only downside is these people can attract more dominant reds and blue aura people to them.

Light Yellow

Is often very spiritual. Make fantastic healers.

The yellow energy at this level is very pure all most un-tainted; there will be innocence about how they view life.

Can be very idealistic and might not live in the real world.

But would be a joy to live with as life would be very simple.

Would have few processions. Wouldn't value money.

Purple

Beware of purple auras.

These people would like to think of themselves as being somebody they are not.

Don't have the ability to find their own way, will be at-tached to other people's ideas or teachings.

Repeating knowledge rather than instigating what they might think.

Often loners who don't fit in socially.

Can be very controlling of others hiding behind helping.

On the plus side if you see a strong purple aura try to remember not to get too close.

Violet

The same as above with a little less intent.

Violet people tend to keep themselves to themselves.

Will not have personal opinions but adopt opinions of others.

Easily lead, but will often form friends with stronger dark blues.

Not that good in social situations.

Frustrated communicators.

Dark Brown

Is the nearest you will see to black in an aura.

Changeable to extreme moody, difficult often intent worrying about what they can't achieve.

Can get involved with addiction in order to find something that excites or helps them forget.

Will make the same mistakes over and over again.

Beware of Dark Brown, at work they tend to be bullies.

Brown

Not good at communicating.

Will eat to feel better.

People who are unhappy and then eat to change their moods will be brown.

The emotional difficulties will show in the weight of the person.

Light Brown

On the edge of wanting to be different.

Light brown can be highlighted with light yellow which indicates the person could go either way depending on the people they surround themselves with.

Lots of promise to be realised or could go the other direction and become lacking in responsibility.

Dark Grey

Lacking sleep.

This person's energy has been drained by a long emotional batter with people close to them.

Can show unwell in areas of the body.

When Grey replaces more vibrant colours, it means the energy isn't being replaced.

Light Grey

Is temporary just shows that the person is tried at that moment.

Could be they haven't eaten for a few hours. If you see light grey with holes in the outer orange aura, it means that the person is at the beginning of a virus or has had a long period of hard work or study.

White

The pureness of aura energy, untainted.

You will see clear energy around people's inner aura, but its normally only reserved for very young babies.

Once life starts to become more involved the white aura will start to give out pale blues and light pinks.

What we must always remember is that the aura is made up from three parts (outer, middle, and inner) it is very rare just to see one colour.

But what you do get are dominant colours.

These are the colours you are looking for.

The overlapping colours can sometimes give you a false impression, so look out for the middle aura this is where you will get the best indication to the person's personality.

The inner aura closest to the skin is light white or grey, inside these area's you will see what the person has been eating or even any injures the person might be surfing from.

Sportsmen and women are good to look at their inner aura for signs of wear in the legs and shoulders.

The outer aura is orange

But can be seen with the blues, reds and greens affecting the shade of the orange. If the outer aura is wearing thin or has gaps in this is an indication that the person isn't looking after themselves, either pushing too hard or not allowing enough time for recovery or taking an artificial aid like pain killers or caffeine.

Different colours show this very clearly.

Aura Wisdom

Want more? Then give more.

Chapter Five: Matching Aura

No longer do we have to be just beautiful on the inside, we can be beautiful on the outside too.

Understanding the colours that people show from their aura can remove the risk of getting involved with people who don't enhance the way we are.

We no longer have to pretend to fit.

We can be who we really are.

This has the power to change the way you live and the people who you choose to live your life with.

No longer do you need others to accept you, because you accept yourself for who you are on the inside.

No more doing things because we believe if we don't, others won't either, but overall by being a person who can read others you can see for yourself what the real meaning of true colours is.

When we believe in ourselves, we don't need to be needed, we find contentment in the moment.

How do we choose the people we want to be friends with?

Do we leave it to chance?

Allow others to approach us?

Far safer to be chosen rather than be the chooser, no fear of rejection.

We tend to fear what we don't know.

Not many of us fully understand the opposite sex.

So are good friendships stroke relationships just down to fate and luck?

And if they are, do we achieve good results by allowing others to do all the decision making especially in the first few hours of a potential relationship?

You could believe that you might get lucky, or we may think that we never meet the right people. Either way you could be right.

Matching auras can give us the edge when it comes to stepping up and making the first move.

We still might fear rejection, this is normal, but if we make our choices on how we see somebodies aura then we can eliminate the worry of falling for a pretty face or charming words.

Having come this far, you will know the importance of self.

Aura: Life in 4D

Get it right from a personal direction then the rest of life's harder decisions become simple.

How we feel on the inside will show out in our aura.

What we tell ourselves will occur; I remember this in one phrase "Thoughts become things".

The difference we feel once we get our thinking right is remarkable.

I see aura's around people who have been told time and time again that they can't.

This sort of tape running over and over again in your mind is enough to stop anyone thinking that life could be easier.

So begin with your own personal thoughts.

Positive mental attitude is the foundation of getting your aura right.

Put the tapes in your mind away. They haven't worked for you in the past so why would you want to keep listening?

Changing your thoughts can be scary at first, that fear again!

But think of it this way.

Every day you walk to work, or to the shops, the shoes you have are old but very comfortable, in the sole are a few holes but on dry days you never notice as your feet feel great.

Then it rains the water comes in and your feet feel wet and cold.

The discomfort is only just bearable, but who knows tomorrow will be sunny again you will forget how you felt on that cold wet day until the next time it rains.

So in your wisdom one day after having cold wet feet for the last time you decide to buy a brand new pair of shoes. At first the heel rubs and your toes feel cramped up, they are hard to get used to and then without noticing your feet start to feel great.

No pitching or rubbing just easy to wear, you have made the change, gone through the pain of accepting, now you're feeling the benefits and walking becomes a pleasure again.

The first step of facing change is always the hardest step.

Every single thing we do in life starts with one single thought.

We first have to realise that we need to change. If we get by in the difficult times, we will accept that life is that way.

Positive mental thinking will take us away from a negative way of thinking. Our thoughts will become positive our mind will start to realise when things are wrong making the choices earlier is the only way forward.

People who have this way of thought have clear energy in their auras.

Again it's not what we have been through it's how we are now that counts.

If you let past mistakes overwhelm you then you may stay in the fear of making more bad decisions.

What this in turn will do is leave you in one place not making choices just accepting your lot as it is.

You can change this by thought. Just the fact that you have thought about this is enough to start a new way of thinking. It's that simple.

Your aura will reflect this. It's like dominoes once we start by pushing the first brick over we can't stop.

Now you don't have to accept my word for it there is a little experiment you can do for yourself.

I believe how we are thinking shows out from the energy that surrounds us.

Next time you go out try walking with your head down, shuffling along not noticing anyone, not talking or smiling, just head down.

Do whatever you have to do then return home.

(This is what most of us do when we have our minds on other things, our aura becomes tightly wrapped around us and we become unapproachable, how many people have you seen today that are hidden behind mobile phones, newspapers, M.B.3 players, you don't need to read their aura to stay away)

Now try the same journey as before but this time pick your head up, look around above your eye level, smile at people, maybe stop and talk to a few shopkeepers.

Your whole experience changes because of your attitude.

This one simple thing can demonstrate that once we remove the negative thoughts or the fear our whole life changes.

We meet others who are feeling like us (like attracts like) what we send out from our aura makes the life that we live.

Every single day we have choices to make when meeting people, but the first choice we make long before we step out of our front door, is - how are we going to be "when"? Don't let fear control the "when" moment.

Aura: Life in 4D

Everything we are starts with a single thought.

From the moment we wake up to what we choose to wear, to the breakfast we eat to the transport we use and the job we do.

We never ever think of our lives as a cascade of decisions but it is.

Make good choices and we benefit, make bad ones and we learn, don't make a choice and we stay in the same place.

Your aura will reflect this. Learning to read other people's auras will help you avoid the stuck person who wants others to make their choices, decisions for them. The aura is a giveaway because it will be tightly moulded to them, but you might have to look out for the other signs too.

These people will only be interested in you in the first instance.

Mainly talking about how they feel without listening.

Will talk about life in an idyllic way.

How they wished things were.

Would be good at putting you at your ease, coming across non-threatening even friendly, though you wouldn't have met before.

People who come in fast like this are scared.

Scared that you may find them out.

Once you have their aura in your view, this will confirm how tight the energy is.

The colours to look out for are dark browns and dark blues, with middle aura energy leaking out of the orange outer aura; gaps around the head and tummy areas will just confirm this person has little of their own energy.

Stay around this person too long and you will feel drained.

All these signs will help you avoid long term contact.

Every day is an opportunity to measure yourself against your own potential, your potential to make the right choices in the people that you invite into your life.

By first understanding how your aura attracts others, then interpreting their aura can in turn give you the confidence to make the correct choices.

We know how we feel. Our emotions act as indicators of the moment. Happy or sad, our inner feelings will affect our outward behaviour.

Our moods are for others easy to pick up on.

Aura: Life in 4D

For every single feeling, mood or emotion there is a colour that shows up in our aura.

Being able to see and interpret these colours is the very first step to understanding others; this in turn will help us create the best possible relationships.

By being able to see in others what we are looking for, we are not relying on what we hear, or more like it what we want to hear.

We will make our own judgements by what we see.

Take this alongside our own personal intuition how could we fail but to form long lasting relationships? Getting our own aura right is the first step in attracting others with good auras.

So remember "like attract like".

Just because you see the colours around others doesn't mean you don't have to work on your own emotional issues.

Everything starts with self.

The better we feel, the easier good choices become.

Good relationships start with good choices.

We have to know what we want before we can tell others.

If we rely on people coming to us, all we will meet are people who are easy to meet.

That might sound like all we want, believe me it isn't.

Knowing our own mind, then our own visions then the colours that show from us we can meet people who have the same thinking.

Where we can go wrong is waiting for the right person to bump into our life. By chance. I like to think of this as No chance! No chance of making it past the first few weeks.

The people we meet when we don't do the work ourselves are very often people who are needy or emotionally damaged.

As they don't have a big neon sign above their heads showing us all their past history, we have to rely on picking up the signals.

Aura's can really help us, as long as we don't switch off the intuition we were born with.

The first impression of a person is how they look. Then the smile, closely followed by the voice.

Believe it or not but the smell of the person affects how we see them too.

What is said is often forgotten, but the emotional, personal feel isn't.

So the first thing to remember is not to focus on the words.

People say what they think we want to hear.

The first contact should be about flirting, fun, enjoying the attention without taking it too seriously.

You may never see this person again so why worry (often we are too concerned about meeting a partner to look too deep. As long as we are hearing what we want to hear this person must be right!)

Then we worry this person might not like us or have the same intentions or agenda's as we do. If we don't act fast, we may miss out.

All this is wrong thinking.

Let me explain.

Genuine people will always act with consideration. Your needs will be front and centre of their thoughts. Acting fast wouldn't appeal.

They would want to know about you. It's not enough just to be there.

You will have to take part.

Answer questions. Not just listen.

Your skills at picking out the colours can give you an advantage.

If you can't see the aura that's fine, look at the clothes.

Clothes are the first indication of how people are feeling. (The following is only true when people get to choose what they are wearing, working clothes or uniforms are very deceptive)

Starting from black and working down the scale through greys then whites. Reds, blues, yellows, greens all have meanings.

You are very likely to see these colours in their aura; people are seventy percent unconscious thinkers.

So when this person got dressed for a social event it would be driven by how they were feeling about the time ahead.

Dressing in black shows a need to be in the background, not to be noticed.

Black top is don't look at my tummy, or my chest.

Black trousers aren't so meaningful.

We normally look at the top half of a person.

But when all black is worn together it indicates "I feel bad", don't look at me.

Not many extroverts wear all black unless it's making a statement or being part of a peer group.

People with auras that are dark tend to choose dark clothing.

Black in an aura is about not being able to deal with emotional past issues, or might have concerns about health, or even at extreme be controlling negative half empty people. On a less of level be lacking in self-confidence.

Not making choices. Making others responsible for how they are feeling.

As in any walk of life people who wear a mixture of colours have a balance in how they are feeling. Combinations of reds, whites, yellows, blues greens are all good indications that the person has a personality that is lively, issues about their emotional feelings will still be in the background, but the likely hood is they won't live their life looking for others to take responsibility for their feelings.

It's not what they have been through it's where it has lead them to.

Remember combinations of colours are good.

All one colour can show a lack of balance.

I have already talked about black; this is what the other colours mean.

White. Dressing all in white in the western world means the person is very confident on the surface.

Wants others to notice their body.

Will often have very little to offer in a conversation.

It's enough for these people just to sit back and let others do the work.

Reliant on how they look to attract others.

Red. Dressing all in red means different things depending on gender.

Men don't often wear just red. Red is reserved in male dressing to make a statement. A hanky in the top pocket, or a pair of bright red socks. (Men that do this are secretly trying to break free of a dull existence) Women who want to attract will wear a red dress.

But it's not about finding a partner. Most women who choose red are normally in very happy relationships. They want to tell the world how happy they are.

So attracting people to talk to is a good way of sharing.

Blue. People who choose blue are communicators. So many different shades of blue, the most of any of the colours we wear.

By choosing to wear different shades together it sends out signals of being able to listen but also that we are friendly, non-aggressive.

Blue jeans have become the choice of many because of the non-confrontational signal that we just want to get on with others. A relaxed way of dressing and thinking.

Green. Very few of us choose to wear green.

Just by that very fact those who do want to stand out. It's about making a statement, "I stand for".

People who go through emotional bad break ups will buy green as a sign that they are going to get on with life.

Many will do this but most believe they can't.

Green can also be deemed to be aggressive by others. Just have a look around when you go out not many choose green.

Yellow. The brave and the bold.

Yellow wearers just don't mind what others think.

Strong, opinionated people with something to share.

Like being noticed, like people asking their opinions.

Good communicators, good business people with new ideas.

The colours we choose are very tell-tale. How we think what we want can all be seen through the colours that we wear.

Reading another person's aura can tell us so much about who they are. Once we stop listening we can make our decisions based on what we are seeing.

In this chapter, I have made two strong statements.

"Like attract like".

So before you start looking at others take a good look at yourself.

Deal with the past first.

Don't overlap emotional lives.

By changing your thinking, you are changing your aura.

This will attract people who can enhance your life.

The second point is don't make others responsible for your happiness.

Be selfish.

Aura: Life in 4D

Think about what you want from somebody who wishes to share their life with you.

Look at the colours first.

There will be plenty of time in the future to listen to each other.

One last thing. We have forgotten that relationships are FUN.

Life is not complicated.

People are!

Keep it simple don't be too fast to rush into another's life.

Enjoy the chase.

But most of all enjoy life.

We normally find what we are looking for when we stop looking.

Enjoy the moment.

Aura Wisdom

The only true judge of you is you.

Chapter Six: Photographic Auras

Wanting to read an aura is one thing.

Being able to is something that we all can do with practise and patience.

The harder we work the easy it becomes.

If we are not people watchers before we start learning about auras, we will soon become so.

I will spend many hours watching people.

Looking at their auras, watching their actions.

Often the colours will show intent.

Most of what we do we never think about.

When was the last time you thought about how you walk or breath?

Body language can tell us much about how people are, even the Chinese art of face reading which goes back hundreds of years can give us clues to what lays beneath.

But auras don't lie. Cannot be manipulated.

The energy we give out of our bodies is showing the world everything we are.

People watching is a good way of learning the meanings of the colours.

But there is another way.

Every time a photograph is taken it captures the energy that is the aura.

A freeze frame of a moment in time.

The Aborigine in Australia believes that when a photograph is taken a part of their soul is captured.

This isn't far from the truth.

What a photograph will show us is how the person was at the moment in time the photograph was taken.

Learning how to read the colours captured in the frame can be a valuable asset in understanding how that person was feeling and even thinking when that photograph was taken.

So how do we start to understand photographs?

Aura reading is about focus. The more we look, the more we see.

Photographs are no different.

To start with I would recommend a large colour photograph of just one person A4 is a good size. (You will move on to more complicated photos in time but first let's get your eyes and mind tuned into the process.)

First choose a darkened room, no natural direct light, so draw the curtains.

Not pitch black just enough light to see the objects in the room with you.

Close your eyes for about thirty seconds. This will help you eliminate the light from your eyes before you look at your photograph.

Now open both eyes and focus on the middle of the face, the nose is a good place to start.

Move your eyes to the top of the head just above the hair line, this might take you a few goes but stick with it. The first light you will see is a white outline this should extend around the head line.

This is normal. All colours come from white light. After a few minutes this light will split into colours, what you are looking for is the pale orange on the edge of the white outline.

It's so frustrating at first. I have taught people to read photographs, but the first few times can send your eyes wild.

Aura: Life in 4D

People who have learnt often say it's like looking at those 3d puzzles that once you have the focus right pop right out of the page, reading photographic auras is very similar, but in a room with only indirect light. Once you start seeing the aura you will be hooked.

Now you can see the colours that surround the person in the frame you can move on to different types of photographs.

You will start to see photographic images everywhere you look.

Newspapers are a good sauce of many different types. If you want to practise, have a look through a glossy magazine full of celebrities.

Remember there are only a few rules.

Choose a photograph that is easy to see the head, a dark background helps.

Then close your eyes focus on what you're going to do, open your eyes fix your stare at the middle of the person and slowly move your glance out to the edge of the person in the photo.

What you are looking for is the outline around the person.

Remember the white light you will first see should split into the different colours.

I have found the knowledge of the colours to be the base of understanding of the photograph aura reading.

Because the aura is made up from three different layers, the inner aura is the first area you will see.

The middle aura is often a primary colour, blue, red, green, or a combination of all three in different shades.

The orange outer aura or shell will have different shades of orange.

This will be weaker in some areas and in some cases holes can be seen with colours from the middle aura leaking out.

Gaps in the outer aura are not that common, but you will notice them first because of the darker mixture of colours leaking from the worn, torn, or thinning shell which is the orange outer aura.

A guide to the meaning of the colours will help you.

I have generalised the meanings to keep them simple and easy to understand when you first start looking at then reading aura's from photographs.

A blue or purple inner aura is that of a communicator, the lighter the blue, the better at communication the person is.

As red mixes into the blue to form purple, the more frustrated the person has become with the lack of understanding others show them.

This is an indication of a person who is struggling to get their views over.

A red middle aura is an unhappy person with many issues of mixed emotions.

Coming out to lighter shades of pinks which are typical of a person who needs to be valued, will trust easily, and even fall in love without much thought.

Green is all about the foods we eat, the pace of our bodies. Brighter greens indicate caffeine artificial stimulants.

These are the basic meanings of the primary colours.

I have gone into more details about the meanings of the different shades in (Meaningful Colours.)

Once you have mastered the meanings you will start to see trends, familiarity between people who are surrounded by the same colours.

You might even find that your friends share more in common than they know.

We are attracted to the same colours often even though we look at people by how they talk and dress.

Photographic aura reading will change the way you look at photographs and in turn the people in your life.

With so many different ways of looking at auras "the photograph "holds a record of how that person or people were feeling at the time of the photograph was taken.

Even black and white photos have an energy that surrounds the images inside. It's different shades of grey but you can see how bright or if the outer aura is thin or has holes, as we already know its orange it's just a matter of translating the different shades of grey into orange.

I have also noticed that when you look at a photograph the aura fades as the person grows older and eventually dies. So very old photographs hold onto very little of the energy, it evaporates as the person moves over to spirit.

This is also true of people who have died young.

Colour photographs are brilliant for making connection into spirit.

The photograph works like a window to the soul of the individual, storing information for the reader to translate.

For myself working as a medium, photographs allow me to link with the person, I know by the depth of the aura whether the person is alive or has passed over, which in turn can help me make the link into spirit.

By understanding photographic aura reading then learning about how to translate the information stored, you too can link into the individual energy of the person you are looking at, and it could help you through personal experience to see that the only truth is life after life.

Aura Wisdom

Contentment is a state of mind.

Chapter Seven: Better Relationships

We all want better relationships, whether it's with people we call family, friends or work colleagues and ultimately the person we choose to share our most intimate time with.

Understanding how others feel is the key to unlocking the knowledge of successful outcomes.

We all have the capability to make life so straightforward we wouldn't even notice that we are getting it right.

(It's only when we get life decisions wrong that we suffer the consequences)

So where do we start?

It's simple. Being able to understand yourself is the beginning.

Knowing your own limits, and understanding why you are feeling a certain way.

Your personal aura can indicate how you're going to feel long before your body shows you. Learning to read your own colours will give you a head start.

You will start to see how certain foods can affect your moods.

As an aura reader, I can see the effect of eating meat or sugar has on the way we feel.

The aura becomes middle heavy, protruding from the stomach, reds and crimsons tinted with greens and blacks.

Alcohol shows up as gaps around the back, big dark grey clouds seep from the lower back, caffeine has a similar effect. I see greens running up and down the whole body, thus making the body work twice as fast as it would normally.

(People who drink caffeine tend to have gaps in the orange outer aura.)

This is an indication that the person is worn down, tired, looking for artificial stimulation, not eating the correct foods.

The human body evolved from our ancestors, the hunter-gatherers.

The food we eat today has no relation to that of the first humans. Keep diet simple, it will help you achieve a more content emotional level, which in turn will bring more consistency in your relationships.

The people who talk to me about problems within relationships always mention that they don't know where they stand.

This is because the people they choose to share with have a balance in their emotional thinking. This can be seen in the aura if we look.

It's not too hard because it's the outer aura we need to read.

Once we have focused on the orange outer shell, we should see a solid glow of orange about two centimetres thick.

With people who are emotionally damaged what we will see is small leaks of aura energy around the side of the head and round the tummy area.

This is a sign that the person is fearful of giving too much of their own personal energy.

Let me explain the significance of this.

When we first meet a person we form our opinions by how that person looks, talks and their body language.

Emotionally damaged people are the easiest people to meet.

"They meet you".

You won't have to do too much to attract them. I have come across people who mistakenly think because a person is telling them everything they want to hear the person must be a soul mate.

Wrong. Just one look at the aura will show you the reason the person is so easy to be with is because they have other agenda's.

They need your energy. Their aura's leaking energy and the only way to get the energy back is by draining yours. These people are fast in, and fast out.

Here are a few pointers when looking to find the right person.

We have so many pre-conceived ideas about relationships.

We all have visions of our ideal partners, how they should look, act, talk and behave.

Hidden agendas tend to rule how we feel, but knowledge will help us see through the fake people who we meet, sorting out who is for real and who is trying to pull the wool over our rather tired eyes.

The first meeting.

This is a time when we try to assess the person by communication, exchanging self-disclosure, body language and physical attraction.

Then we have the invisible signs such as smell and even hormones which may make an impact.

If we can navigate past all these areas, then we can get down to finding out whether the person sat opposite, is the real deal or just out to talk a good relationship.

The three questions that we all have to drop casually into conversation are:

1. How did your last relationship end (hoping that the person has a sincere answer without blaming their ex)?

2. How many close friends do you have? This indicates how loyal the person is and how much time and effort they put into remaining close to others.

People with few friends often fall out with those closest to them when difficulties arise; this is not good, as is having too many friends.

On average, five close friends are enough for most people to cope with.

This allows you to meet these people and get another view on what you have been told by your date.

If the person has no friends then be very careful, you don't want to be the only person in the life of your partner, you might end up being responsible for that person's happiness.

3. How do you get on with your family?

Upbringing is so very important, it indicates whether the person has good role models or a bad image of what relationships can be.

The sooner you ask these questions, the sooner you will feel able to relax with your potentially new partner or decide to move on to the next person before getting attached.

Once you are attached to a person, then it's visions that matter.

If you want the same things then you will stay together.

If you have hidden agendas then this is the time to open up and trust your judgement.

People who wish for the same things will never use the line "I don't know what I want".

This line is a way of hiding that they don't want what you want. Believe me people are very quick to agree when they feel the same, don't be fooled.

A guide to the time-scales are as follows:

Honeymoon period. 12 - 16 weeks. Can't get enough of each other.

Visionary period. 16 - 32 weeks. Both feel the same and want the same things.

Together. 32 weeks onwards. This is the time when plans become joint, moving in together, planning a life of the same needs, wants and commitments.

One last thing, always remember that above everything else relationships should be fun. Those who laugh together stay together.

Look at the aura first. Learn to read what that person is before getting involved. This could save you so much time in wasted relationships.

Match auras then you will know that you both want the same things without ever having to talk about it.

Aura Wisdom

If it doesn't matter tomorrow, it shouldn't matter today.

Chapter Eight: Spiritual Auras

How we think is what we become.

Whether or not you believe in the above statement your aura will reflect how you are thinking and feeling.

To have a positive aura and in turn attract others with similar thinking is the purpose of wanting a life where people want to be with us for who we are, not for what we can do for others.

Thinking on a positive level is a way of life, it isn't something we can switch on and off from when it suits us.

The first step to having a positive aura is just a thought away.

Put whatever you have learnt to the back of your mind, and today you're going to start your new way of thinking. A way that nobody has ever had a say in. So all the people that you have welcomed into your life, all of who have opinions about you, don't count anymore, this is about your own opinions.

We all see ourselves different from how others see us.

We worry that we might not be accepted or our bodies are not what others would want to look at.

This is the age we are growing up in, cosmetic surgery for a quick fix.

If we don't like our body it can be altered, if we have enough money.

I look around at the people in the street, every single person can send out whatever image they want.

Young girls with long blonde hair, eyelashes that leap out from underneath painted eyes, all false just to be liked, thinking more about how others would like to see them.

Why do people want to all look the same?

Is it safety in numbers?

Or have we all fallen for the adverts.

No wonder we all want to be told how good we look, it's because we are not sure we do.

The ironic thing is everybody is too busy thinking and worrying how they look to even notice you.

Our personal identity is so much more than how we look. How many of us can look beyond the person and see the truth behind the disguise.

Aura reading will give this.

But first you have to change the way you think and feel about yourself.

We have already discussed positive mental attitude, and the affect your thinking has on who you are, and in turn how others become attracted to you.

If we disguise ourselves behind who we want to be our aura will show this and guess what we will attract false people into our lives.

Looking good and feeling good can be totally different things.

This is why your first step to a positive aura is to look good for yourself.

Being "you" will allow you to see yourself as others do.

This is a big advantage.

As the people who will approach you are more likely to be suited to your way of thinking. (Think false, attract false)

Remember your thinking has been given to you by previous experiences that's why wiping clean your past thoughts will allow you not to get caught up by judging others by past thinking.

Your mind and aura are now in the moment.

You're in control.

You don't have to be the listener or the helper to be able to make friends, you don't need others to tell you how wonderful you look because you are feeling wonderful, reading the aura's around you will just confirm what you are feeling. People are now interested in you, the real you.

You don't mind answering questions, no need to run and hide behind helping others or being the listener, you can be yourself.

Your energy will grow, self-confidence will follow, you now know what has been holding you back.

It's just a matter of thinking.

From the day we are born, we are meeting people.

Our aura's start off white just like a clean page before you get to write on it, only it's not just you doing the writing everyone gets a chance of adding their bit.

The art is to understand that you and you alone need to be the pen holder.

The people we meet have a huge influence on our aura.

The person we become is in part made up of those who have been with us.

But do we choose these souls to be part of our human experience or is it just by chance - do we really have soul mates?

And if we do how do we find them?

This is how I have come to understand the concept of soul mates.

Each one of us has a soul.

This is made up from pure energy (that's why the aura is a reflection of our soul.)

The human soul is divided into segments; one soul is made up from eleven segments.

Each one of us has at least one soul segment within us.

This is our soul energy.

At any one time, there can be another ten segments from our soul living in other people. (Soul mates)

Our soul group is made up from eleven complete souls, eleven x eleven segments, 121 segments of souls. Once you have got your mind around the maths it becomes very simple.

In our life, we will interact on different levels with different people.

But the people we get closest to will be the people from the same soul group.

Our soul mates share the same soul as us, these segments of soul would have interacted across many lifetimes together.

The knowledge of each other is total.

This is why when you meet a person with a segment of your shared soul the attraction is such a strong one a relationship becomes unavoidable.

This can explain why people fall in love at first sight.

It's not first sight, it's reconnecting to a part of yourself, a part that would know everything you ever have experienced as a soul.

I have spoken to many couples who have experienced a soul relationship.

I believe these relationships are very common; the majority of us will experience soul relationships during our lifetimes.

The soul sends out a frequency that vibrates at a certain level.

This is what we pick up on; it's like blue electricity being passed from one segment of soul to the other.

When you see soul mates together, the aura will vibrate at the same pitch. I have heard people saying "we are just in tune with one another".

This is truer than they know.

When people say to me I want to find my soul mate, the first thing I will reply is sort out your aura by fixing the way you think and feel.

This is because if the aura is full of negative thought energy or others draining your aura because you thought by helping others with their problems it was a quick way to a relationship.

How can our soul mates sense the aura they are looking for?

An aura weighed down with emotional worry, (i.e.) self-esteem issues, will never vibrate on its natural level. That's why when we look after ourselves first, others who want to be with us soon follow.

It's so important to get your aura right not only for your own well-being but also because it's the beacon that allows your soul mates to find you.

You can make this happen, try it for yourself it's only a thought away.

Meditation is a great starting place if you're looking to control your conscious thinking.

Most people who I teach meditation start by telling me that they can't meditate.

They have tried and failed.

That's fine by me at least they know what it involves.

But by the very nature of the failing they have been drawn to something they know nothing about, haven't taken the time to learn in order to experience.

I have a different approach when it comes to teaching meditation.

I believe that personal experience is the only way to gain knowledge.

So if you would like to follow my teaching regarding meditation, please read on.

Our everyday life is split up into different sections.

- We have family time.
- Work time.
- Eating time.
- Relaxation time.
- Sleep time.

Working out how much of this time is spent on you this is your first step.

Your routine is something you will never step far away from.

Next you will need to put aside thirty minutes to watch television by yourself.

That's not too hard; most of us have a time in our day that we watch certain television programmes.

When we become engrossed, nothing will stop us from watching.

Our mind is totally focused on the T.V.

We might hear noise in the background, we might see others moving around in the same room but our focus is straight in front.

From the title music at the beginning to the closing credits at the end our attention is the happenings on the screen.

All your thoughts and worries have been replaced by what you're watching.

What you have been doing is meditation.

So do you still think you can't do it?

Now all we have to do is recreate this for you.

Whatever you need to become focused. It might be that you need a visual focus point.

A photograph of a garden, or the universe, even a sunset, something that can catch your mind and envelop you within it.

The next thing to consider is your sense of smell.

Smell always triggers thoughts; think about childhood smells like the fairground this always brings memories flooding back.

Use a scented candle or an oil burner with a scent you feel drawn to.

Use the same scent every time you meditate, your mind will relate the smell to meditation.

So now we have two senses working with us- now for your ears.

I have found bird song is very relaxing during meditation, but you may choose something totally different.

Now focus on the visual imagine until your eyes start to close.

See the same image inside your mind, take yourself as if you were walking amongst the photograph, let your nose smell the scent, let your imagination take over, you can now fly or swim it's up to you, this is your world make of it what you want.

Now you have your special place start to bring in things that you like to be surrounded with.

When I first learned to meditate I would climb up the stone staircase inside my hollow oak tree till I reached the top where there was an old wooden door which would open onto a lush green meadow.

As I entered the emerald green field, I smelt the air, heard the bees buzzing and the birds singing around my head.

The flowers were bright shades of yellows and reds; this meadow is a place I wanted to be in.

I even personalised my meadow by planting a sapling, a young apple tree.

This is my special place, I spend an hour a day under my tree, and it has become a meeting place.

My guides will sense when I'm going to be there and wait for me, I could spend hours with them if time existed in my meditation world.

Till this day, I still sit under my now ageing tree, eating its juicy green apples whilst listening to my spirit guides.

This is the world I have created for myself.

You too can create your own meditation.

Starts with a single thought.

Aura Wisdom

If you can think it, you can do it.

Chapter Nine: New Knowledge

How do you think? Have you ever thought about thought?

I love finding out new knowledge.

I question everything even where the thought came from in the first instance.

Just think you are now reading this book, and getting to this stage is a small miracle, all the different circumstances that had to happen just for you to read the words right in front of you.

How we think has a major say on how our lives progress.

But how do we come to make the decisions we do?

What prompts us to choose the red coat rather than the brown one?

Do all our thoughts come just from us?

And how does our aura affect our thoughts or is it our thoughts that affect our aura?

This is what I have come to believe after much thought!

Our thoughts influence everything we do.

But long before we think about doing something the seed has already been planted deep inside our subconscious.

From the colours we choose to wear, to the food we decide upon to eat, are all thoughts planted long before we even noticed we were able to make conscious choices.

Our bodies send us certain signals that our brains pick up from.

So straight away we have two inside influences that affect our actions, and this is before we explore our five senses.

To understand this, we may have to change the way we have been taught by others.

Even question why we have been taught in a certain way.

In fact, ever since we first drew breath, the people who have cared for us, taught us and even hurt us have all made their mark on how we think.

To open up our thinking we first have to understand how many different layers are involved.

I believe that our thoughts don't just come from us.

Our past lives, future lives have all left us with certain knowledge.

This knowledge can come out in areas such as phobias or even certain relationships.

It appears that the more emotional the past life, memories of that lifetime are the nearer to the surface, allowing us a tiny glimpse when we go through a traumatic experience in our current life, (for some reason emotionally charged experiences trigger these past life memories or thoughts rather like playing a tape back) normally through our dreams.

But these thoughts although influential don't seem to have been part of the lifetime we are living.

To put this in perspective try and think back to a vivid dream.

Then think back to what had happened to you the day before.

Once you can join up the two then this knowledge will change the way you will look at personal experiences.

For me, it's good to know that you can access all the knowledge that has ever been learned.

That somehow knowledge is either stored inside you or the universe holds every conscious thought that has ever been thought ready for you to access.

(Clairvoyance universal knowledge) is the way the spiritualists explain this, or cell memory as the past life believer thinks.

But basically it's the same thing.

It means that we can pick up thoughts from other areas than just our own thoughts. I have always seen things a little differently from mainstream thinking, but however you come across this it's well worth exploring.

As always keep an open mind, personal experience is the only way to change your own belief structures that is unless your thoughts are being sent to you.

Auras are a great way to explore the real person behind the thoughts.

When we first grow and start creating our own personality our aura will grow with us.

Up to around the age of seven the aura is very white with touches of orange and red and blues in the outer aura.

Because the aura is the true reflection of who we are other people don't get to change these colours, but as we grow others become more influential on who we become, and we start to form opinions, understanding our own personal likes or dislikes, feel emotions, and can easily fall in love.

Remembering who we were as a child can really help us in adulthood. Our identity is formed before our eighth birthday, the character that we carry into our adult life is already opening up but unlike as we get older life is very simple, it's easy to be true to who we want to be.

No constraints, like money, responsibilities, and relationships, just uncomplicated days.

As we get older and start choosing our own peer groups, our minds and thoughts get taken over by the thinking of others.

We join in following certain music, or choose to be involved in sports, but what we are doing is finding safety in numbers, being a part of a group is far safer than going out on our own.

Our aura will reflect this; the person that we were is now what others want us to be all because we want to feel safe.

Moving this on you can see when we start to form adult relationships our own individuality has now changed, we need to please others to feel a part of who we think we have become, so we look for partners who need us, can adopt their identity, and in turn we feel safe but in exchange we make our partner responsible for our own happiness. The aura will show us this if we look closely. As couples we often start to take on each other's features.

Sometimes dressing alike, eating the same food, following the same interests and hobbies.

It's only when we start to evolve as people that we will break away from controlling partners.

(This applies especially to younger woman. Girls in their middle teens will try and hook up with an older man. They will feel safe, often focusing on the man's life, this is also good for the man, he isn't questioned, he has total control in the relationship which he wouldn't find with a partner of his own age. The only thing is these relationships don't last. The girl grows up, finds her own mind, feels the need to explore and experience new people. The control at the start of the relationship that was so appealing has now gone, it becomes a prison. The man hasn't changed; the girl has become a woman and doesn't need another person to speak for her.)

This is part of life; from the moment we are born we start to evolve.

The people we meet along the way serve a purpose but once that purpose is through then we move on or become subservient to people who we don't care for any longer. This can turn to anger then in turn manifest into despair. I think of people that we have in our lives in three ways.

The passenger

This is a person who needs us to get where they are going, we will offer as much help as we can, they will take whatever we give them until we decide they have come far enough with us.

Sometimes passengers stay a whole lifetime but only because we can't gather the courage to change or to move on ourselves.

The hitch-hiker

This person only comes along for part of own journey, we choose to pick them up but they choose when they decide to get out. If we fall in love with the hitch-hiker, it can be a relationship that is very hard to get over.

The driver

This person we trust with our hopes and dreams.

We choose to share everything with them placing them in charge of everything we want, need, and wish for. These people will never leave our lives through choice.

We meet all these people at some time during our life - the art is understanding who is who.

Our aura is a giveaway.

It tells others how we are thinking.

I believe this is what attracts others to us.

If we give out the colours that we are looking for, a hitch-hiker this is the person who we will draw to us.

So how we think is not only affecting the colours within our aura it's also helping to manifest the reality that we are thinking of creating.

This is why the correct way of thinking is so important.

If we believe we deserve a kind loving relationship and really think this with no doubt in our minds, this is what we will attract.

Your aura is an extension of your personal thought.

The colours you give out will attract people with the matching colours and thinking.

I was once told the difference between being mortal and being spiritual is impatience.

When we are in spirit all we are is thought, we can manifest in an instant, whatever we want the reality to be we can create with thought.

Not so on planet Earth.

We have to first think, then struggle, search and wait.

No wonder we are impatient, being mortal is a lot more difficult than being spiritual.

We don't need to complicate life.

Keep everything simple.

Love this life, once we start to believe this and live this way it changes everything.

Thought however you come across it, will change the way your life is.

Everything you are has been created by the thoughts that have come through you.

These thoughts might not originate from your mind, but you certainly have adopted them as yours.

Training your thoughts to work with you is the first step forward.

Affirmations are the starting point, when we repeat something daily we will start to see how our thinking changes "I love and approve of myself" is a very simple short one line that we can all say to ourselves whilst cleaning our teeth in the morning and evening.

From the moment we start to feel these words, we start believing that the value we place on ourselves is a high one.

No longer will we attract people who want to control us or put us down because we are not putting our own self down.

Not only won't we believe others who tell us we are not worthy, it is highly likely we won't attract these people into our lives' in the first place.(Needy people have nothing to give us back so the only way they stay in our lives is if they lower our self-esteem)

Thinking positive, acting positive will attract the same positive people to you.

Try it.

People who have positive thoughts will extend their aura way out from their bodies.

All the energy you produce is yours, your aura will glow; you will only feel drained when around people who don't look at life in a positive way.

But boy will you be aware of them.

The mistake some of us make is thinking because people are family we should put up with them, this is wrong.

When a person thinks they can act and say anything they want to us without consequence, they will.

We have no need to accept this behaviour.

Once they realise that we won't make allowances for them they will try to make us feel guilty.

Emotional guilt is one of the hardest emotions that we will face as an adult.

This is because ever since we were born our parents have instilled in us a sense of guilt.

This is mainly to control us without explanation.

Our parents don't know everything and in many cases can't cope with being questioned.

No need to explain if you don't know how to, just make the person feel guilty about asking.

Most of our thinking comes from our parents.

It's only when we realise that they might be wrong or their opinions are not the only ones that we start to think for ourselves.

I think we all should question.

Good parents, friends, work colleagues even lovers won't mind answering our questions when they have a good understanding of why they might be acting the way they are, it's only when they can't explain their actions or words that they will either get angry or hard to communicate with or make us feel guilty just for questioning.

Believe in what you're seeing, peoples actions speak far clearer than any words.

Your knowledge of auras will really help you to see people for what they really are.

True colours can be seen as well as felt.

Aura Wisdom

Your life is shaped by the doors you walk through.

Chapter Ten: Last Word

You have now read just about everything I know about Aura's, the meanings of the colours and how this new knowledge can help you take a fresh look at yourself, people and your relationships.

It has taken me over forty years to form my views on auras, understanding the different colours, working out through experience the different combinations.

How different colours mean different things.

You have had as long as it has taken you to read this book.

My hope is you won't give up if you don't start seeing aura's within the first few hours of trying.

The aura is the missing link between people being able to understand others far better.

Like anything new, it will take you some time to practise.

People who I have taught get a tremendous amount of pleasure especially when they see their first aura.

It opens a whole new world. Seeing is believing.

The understanding of relationships is unique to me. I have never come across another person who thinks or sees life in the same way I do.

I have never had to look too hard to see auras.

Everything is surrounded by colour, even sounds. I have always seen colours through sound.

Voices become a mass of vibrating blues, greens and reds jumping from the mouths of unsuspecting people.

I believe that the colours that come from people are created by the vibrations of our bodies.

Different people vibrate at different frequencies thus creating their own very personal colour signature.

This is the reason I love music so much.

The beautiful colours that come from the human voice still amaze me to this day, piano music is so vibrant in yellows, I could go on, but this world is open to us all if we atone our thinking to the vibration of colour.

From the moment we start to breathe, our aura is being formed.

The control we have over the colours we give out is the way we think.

Thought is so much a part of every single action we ever make during our whole life.

So from the very start we have a record of every single thought we have ever had, these thoughts are built up all around us.

The people who have influenced our thinking, who we think we are, who we want to become, are all shown for all of us who can read then interpret the colours of the aura.

Once we understand that thoughts are everything then we start to change our lives'.

The aura that you have is the force of attraction.

What we think we become, and what we become attracts others to us.

This simple concept is behind all that we do.

Being happy with ourselves is the key to contentment.

This is a way of attracting others.

Needing, wanting and even greed are all forms of tying yourself up in knots.

Be yourself. Find the purpose of your life through yourself, not others. When you try to find your true identity through others, it's like climbing a staircase starting on the sixth stair.

You can do it, but it hurts to get your leg up that high.

Start from the first stair and work your way up, everybody can climb some faster than others but it's not the speed it takes to get to the top it's getting to the top that counts.

We can all find reasons why we can't do something, most of these are mental.

We start believing that we will never reach the top, and guess what we won't.

We have already made an excuse before we start, and when we fail we are just confirming how right we were when we started on this ridiculous quest.

This way of thinking is taught to us by our parents its deep inside our conscious thoughts.

Our parents are our first role models.

The people who we look to for guidance.

We would never question their wisdom.

People who live fulfilling lives have the backing of fulfilled parents.

But when our parents struggle to find their own way forward the most natural thing for them to do is find a focus in others.

They have children, build their world around them, and make the child responsible for the purpose of their lives. So when the child starts to grow and become independent the parent needs to control the child by teaching the child to accept what they themselves accepted long before the child was born.

This is that you can never climb the stairs right the way to the top because they couldn't. (Because the parent couldn't find their own true purpose, and if the child shows that they can it's like a child showing up the inadequacies of the parent)

Not many see this because those of us who have been lucky enough to have truly wonderful parents who teach independence and self-belief would just carry on, attracting others who think and feel the same way.

Whilst those of us who have had parents who have hidden behind caring for us to disguise they own frailties would never question the fact that they couldn't climb the stairs because they wouldn't want to, they already know it can't be done.

So what about the people who see through their parents?

These are the people who tend to fall out with each other.

If a child is successful by their own means, the parent won't want to be reminded of their own failure by seeing a child reaching the top.

And the child won't want to be told they can't do something just because the parent couldn't.

Some things in life are unavoidable, and parents are one of those things.

Emotional guilt is something we are taught by our parents, some of us never get over the way others try to make us feel.

If you recognise all that you have just read, change the cycle, and be the first in your family to look beyond what your parents and very likely their parents have been getting wrong for generations.

Aura's can teach us so much about others.

Where in the past we have relied on words and actions, we no longer have just these two areas we have a third point of reference.

How many people have you met during your lifetime that if you had of known more about their true self would you have got involved with?

Without exception, we all like to think that we can make judgements on others quickly.

Most of us take up to 30 seconds to judge another person.

Relying on our own personal thoughts.

What do we look at to make such snap judgements?

Age?

Hair colour?

Clothes?

Job?

Past experiences with similar looking people?

What the person has to say about themselves?

None of these things count.

All of the above is how that other person wants you to see them.

Could you pick out the policeman from a line of men, or the prisoner from a similar line-up?

I doubt that you could.

So why think you could work out a personality from meeting someone.

It's false thinking.

Reading an aura is like having a look inside a person.

You will have to relearn the way you look at people.

Not be influenced by words or actions, just colours.

Aura Wisdom

Even in the most difficult circumstances you can still grow.

Dominic Zenden
hello@dominiczenden.com
www.dominiczenden.com
Twitter@dominiczenden
Facebook Dominic.J.Zenden

Little miracles happen every day.

Made in the USA
Columbia, SC
10 August 2018